ISBN 1 85103 320 3

Originally published as *Hector Berlioz Découverte des Musiciens* jointly by Editions Gallimard Jeunesse & Erato Disques.
© & ℗ 1998 Editions Gallimard Jeunesse & Erato Disques.
This edition first published in the United Kingdom jointly by Moonlight Publishing Ltd, The King's Manor, East Hendred, Oxon OX12 8JY
& The Associated Board of the Royal Schools of Music (Publishing) Limited, 24 Portland Place, London W1B 1LU.
English text © & ℗ 2002 by Moonlight Publishing Ltd & The Associated Board of the Royal Schools of Music.
Printed in Italy by Editoriale Lloyd.

Hector

BERLIOZ

FIRST DISCOVERY - MUSIC

Written by Christian Wasselin
Illustrated by Charlotte Voake
Narrated by Michael Cantwell

La Côte-Saint-André is a little village in the Dauphiné region of France, between the Alps and the River Rhône. It was there, a few days before Christmas in 1803, that Hector Berlioz was born.

LISTEN TO NATURE

Each season of the year has different natural sounds. The cuckoo calls in spring. In summer you can hear the lark high above the cornfields and sometimes the rumble of thunder. Listen to all these sounds. Record them on a tape recorder and play them back to your friends. Can they tell which season it is?

1 BENVENUTO CELLINI, OVERTURE
FANTASTIC SYMPHONY, 3RD MOVEMENT, 'SCENE IN THE FIELDS'

Inside the house, wood is burning in the fireplace. Outside, the wind is whistling and crows are cawing, but all these sounds are softened by the falling snow.

Hector takes his first communion aged eleven. Girls are singing a religious song in the church. Hector has never heard anything like this before. He is deeply affected

2 THE CHILDHOOD OF CHRIST, 'THE SHEPHERDS' FAREWELL'

by the sound of their voices. From this day on, music is a very important part of Hector's life. Many of his great compositions are religious works.

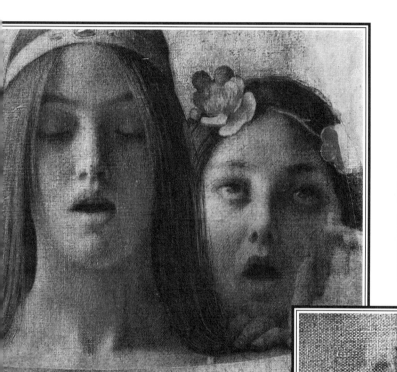

SINGING TOGETHER

A choir is made up of several, sometimes dozens of singers. They all try hard to sing in time and in tune together. With your friends try singing a song or a piece of music which you all know. Even if there are not many of you, you will find that it is not as easy as you may think!

Hector is the eldest of the Berlioz children. His sisters Nanci and Adèle are several years younger than him. Hector's father is a doctor and would like his son to learn to be a doctor too. He is very patient, well-read and well-

A PUFF OF AIR AND A TUBE

The flute has a soft, sometimes happy, sometimes rather sad sound. The way this instrument works is very simple. Try taking an empty bottle and blowing across the rim. You will soon get a sound. If you try with several bottles of different sizes you will get different sounds. If there are a number of you, you could form a wind ensemble!

respected, and teaches Hector science, Latin and how to read music. He also arranges for him to have lessons in flute, guitar and singing. Hector begins to write music and plays his first compositions with his friends.

When he is twelve, Hector falls madly in love with a girl of seventeen, Estelle. Estelle is tall, slim, beautiful and

HAVE YOU EVER DANCED A WALTZ?

In Berlioz's time people used to dance a lot: for birthdays and weddings and at balls. The waltz became fashionable at this time. The boy puts his right hand around the girl's waist and the girl puts her left hand on his shoulder. They hold each other's hand and begin to turn, one, two, three, faster and faster! Listen to this waltz and try waltzing with your brother, your sister or one of your friends.

elegant. She likes dancing with Hector's uncle, who is a soldier. This makes poor Hector feel unhappy. This is the time when the French emperor Napoleon I has just conquered most of Europe.

At the same time as Hector starts to study music, he also learns how to read maps. He dreams of going off on journeys and of becoming a sailor. From his house he can see the Alps. He would like to see further, beyond the

STREET MUSICIANS

In Italy there are travelling musicians, who play from one village to the next. They are called *pifferari*. Berlioz saw and heard some of them. Have you and your friends ever played music in the streets? You could try it at Christmas, a local holiday or other celebration. Go with a grown-up, and choose friends whose instruments are easy to carry – a flute or a guitar. When you are in a group, you become much more daring!

mountains, to Italy. Later on, Hector will become a great traveller and will explore Europe from one end to the other, from London to Russia. But while he is a boy, he can only travel in his dreams.

Hector loves to listen to country people singing as they walk in processions or celebrate harvest festival. When he is seventeen, he begins to compose songs to express his feelings of love and sadness.

SING IF YOU ARE FEELING SAD

Have you ever felt very sad and unhappy? It can be hard to express how you feel. You probably know a sad song. Try singing it, maybe with a friend, when you are sad. You'll feel much better after a really good sing!

Hector is eighteen. He is about to go to Paris. His father wants him to study medicine, but Hector is not sure he wants to be a doctor. He is in love with Estelle. He also loves reading, he wants to travel, and music is never far from his mind. His nights are filled with dreams and nightmares. He is confused by all these strong feelings.

DO YOU ENJOY FEELING SCARED?

Berlioz loved making instruments produce scary or mournful sounds. Sometimes they give the impression of a monster's hollow laugh. Try making a door squeak on its hinges or an attic stair creak. Listen – night has fallen, the wind is whistling, a dog is howling, owls are hooting. Just imagine what scary music you could make using all these sounds!

7 FANTASTIC SYMPHONY, 5TH MOVEMENT, 'DREAM OF A WITCHES' SABBATH'

Today

as in the past

Berlioz's

music

is played

and loved.

THE TROJANS

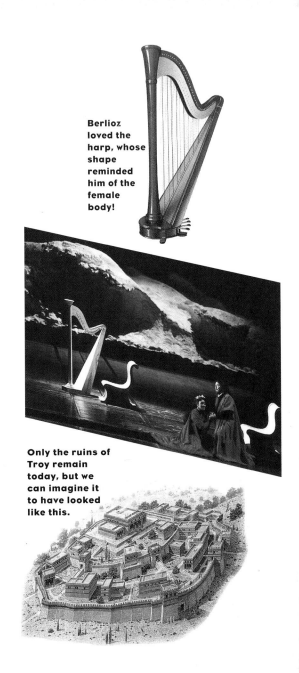

An opera is like a play, but the words are sung by singers instead of spoken by actors. In an opera, an orchestra accompanies the voices. This, when Berlioz is involved, is very colourful. Berlioz wrote some operas which he did not think were good enough, so he burnt them! But he wrote three operas which he did not burn, and they are performed nowadays. One opera is called *The Trojans*. It is based on a Latin poem, *The Aeneid* by Virgil, which Berlioz read when he was a child. All his life Berlioz was influenced by things he learnt in his childhood.

Berlioz loved the harp, whose shape reminded him of the female body!

Only the ruins of Troy remain today, but we can imagine it to have looked like this.

HAROLD IN ITALY

Many composers wrote symphonies and gave them numbers. Berlioz didn't give his symphonies numbers; he gave them titles instead, to make his audience dream and to fire their imaginations. His first symphony is called the *Fantastic Symphony*. In another symphony, *Harold in Italy*, Berlioz describes his memories of Italy. A sad and dreamy-sounding instrument can be heard throughout the work: the viola. Its sound is somewhere between that of a violin and a cello.

The *Fantastic Symphony* is like a musical novel without words, in which Berlioz tells you about the woman he loves.

Later he recounts how his love has plunged him into nightmares.

FANTASTIC SYMPHONY, 4TH MOVEMENT, 'MARCH TO THE SCAFFOLD'
HAROLD IN ITALY, 2ND MOVEMENT, 'PILGRIM'S MARCH'

THE CHILDHOOD OF CHRIST

Berlioz first discovered music through nature and religion. In his music he liked to give the impression of vast space and a feeling of freedom, and also of intimate places, where people could turn to their innermost thoughts. He always liked his music to show these huge contrasts. In the Requiem very loud music passes into silence. The brass and percussion instruments contrast with pleading voices. In his Te Deum you can hear an organ and a children's choir. His oratorio *The Childhood of Christ* tells the story of how the infant Jesus escaped the Massacre of the Innocents. An atmosphere of great tenderness pervades the music, in which you can sense the landscapes of the Middle East.

The Te Deum was played for the first time in the church of St Eustache in Paris, whose organ is shown in this illustration.

A chapel in the mountains: one of Berlioz's favourite scenes.

THE DAMNATION OF FAUST

Berlioz was a creator of great imagination. He wrote works full of mystery. In *Lélio, or The Return to Life* Berlioz has an actor wake up from a nightmare and address the orchestra and the singers. In *The Damnation of Faust* we are in an imaginary opera! There is no scenery and yet we follow the characters from Hungary to Germany, in a cabaret, at the water's edge, in a bedroom, in a garden, and into the depths of hell. Berlioz was also the first to write compositions for solo voice and full orchestra. Among the most beautiful of these is *Les Nuits d'été* (*Summer Nights*). Berlioz loved to combine the voice with the orchestra. His music is a real celebration in singing and sound.

Percussion instruments are used to evoke storms, hurricanes and earthquakes.

MOONLIGHT PUBLISHING

Translator:
Penelope Stanley-Baker

ABRSM (PUBLISHING) LTD

Project manager:
Leslie East

Language consultant:
Cathy Ferreira

Text editor:
Lilija Zobens

Editorial supervision:
Caroline Perkins & Rosie Welch

Production:
Simon Mathews & Michelle Lau

English narration recording:
Ken Blair of BMP Recordings

ERATO DISQUES

Artistic and Production Director:
Ysabelle Van Wersch-Cot

KEY: **t** = top   **m** = middle   **b** = bottom
        r = right   **l** = left

LIST OF ILLUSTRATIONS

6 Jean Achard (1807–1884), *View of La Dent de Croles, near Grenoble*. The Louvre, Paris. **9** L. W. Hawkins (1849–1910), *Girls Singing a Song by Gabriel Fauré*, around 1903. Private collection. **11** M. D. Oppenheim (1800–1882), *Tutor with his Two Pupils*, around 1830, detail. Deutsches Historisches Museum, Berlin. **13** Charles Wilda (1854–1907), *Joseph Lanner and Johann Strauss*, 1906. Historical Museum of the City of Vienna. **14** Theodor Hosemann (1807–1875), *'Rome', pifferaro*, 1846. Art and History Archives, Berlin. **15** C. D. Friedrich (1774–1840), *Der Watzmann*, 1824. National Gallery, Berlin. **17** Jules Breton (1827–1906), *The Blessing of the Corn in Artois*, 1857. Musée des Beaux-Arts, Arras. **18** J. H. Füssli (1741–1825), *The Nightmare*, about 1790. Freies Dt. Hochstift, Frankfurt. **19** Gustave Courbet (1819–1877), *Portrait of Hector Berlioz*, 1850. Nasjonalgalleriet, Oslo. **20t** Harp. **20m** *The Trojans*, 1990. Opéra National de Paris. **20b** Reproduction of Troy, drawing by Lloyd Townsend. **21** Claude Gelée known as Lorrain (1600–1682), *Landscape, Aeneas at Délos*, 1672. National Gallery, London. **22t** H. Gaugain, *Harriet Smithson*, wife of Hector Berlioz, before 1833. **22m** Shlomo Mintz, violinist and Yuri Bashmet, violist. **22b** Horace Vernet (1789–1863), *The Ballad of Leonora*. Musée des Beaux-Arts, Nantes. **23** William Turner (1775–1851), *Italian Landscape with Mercury*. Christie's, London. **24t** The Organ of Saint-Eustache, Paris. **24m** The Gewandhaus Children's Choir, Leipzig. **24b** Jean Bugnard (1880–1947), *Chapel in the Snow*. Savoy Museum, Chambéry. **25** Giotto (1266–1337), *The Flight into Egypt*, around 1315. Fresco in the Basilica of Assisi. **26t** Théodore Gudin (1802–1879), *Act of Self Sacrifice by Captain Desse of Bordeaux towards the Dutch ship Columbus*, around 1828, detail. Musée des Beaux-Arts, Bordeaux. **26m** Brass and percussion, Orchestre National de Radio-France. **26b** June Anderson, singer. **27** Josef Fay (1813–1875), *Gretchen in Prison*, about 1845. Art and History Archives, Berlin.

PHOTOGRAPHIC ACKNOWLEDGEMENTS

Archiv für Kunst und Geschichte, Paris **9**, **11**, **13**, **14**, **15**, **18**, **19**, **22t**, **25**, **26t**, **27**. Artephot/Martin **21**. C. Thériez. Musée des Beaux-Arts d'Arras **17**. Christie's – Artothek **23**. Jean-Paul Dumontier **24t**. Lloyd Townsend/D. R. **20b**. Musée savoisien, Chambéry **24b**. Ph. Coqueux/Specto **20m**, **22m**, **24m**, **26m**, **26b**. Photo R. M. N. – H. Lewandowski **6**. Photo R. M. N. – P. Bernard **22b**. Pierre-Marie Valat **20t**.

I. One fine December day
Benvenuto Cellini, Op. 23,
Overture
Orchestre Philharmonique
de Strasbourg
Conducted by Alain Lombard
2292 45075 2
℗ Erato Classics SNC, Paris,
France 1973

Symphonie fantastique, Op. 14,
3rd movement, 'Scène aux champs'
Orchestre National de France
Conducted by James Conlon
℗ Erato Classics SNC, Paris,
France 1984

2. First feelings for music
L'Enfance du Christ, Op. 25,
'L'Adieu des Bergers'
Monteverdi Choir
Orchestre de l'Opéra de Lyon
Conducted by John Eliot Gardiner
2292 45275 2
℗ Erato Classics SNC, Paris,
France 1988
Co-production Erato/Cascavelle/
France Musique/Opéra de Lyon

3. Playing music with friends
L'Enfance du Christ, Op. 25,
'Trio des Ismaélites'
Philippe Bernold, Gilles Cottin, flutes
Chantal Mathieu, harp
Solistes de l'Orchestre de l'Opéra
de Lyon
Conducted by John Eliot Gardiner
2292 45275 2
℗ Erato Classics SNC, Paris,
France 1988
Co-production Erato/Cascavelle/
France Musique/Opéra de Lyon

4. In love at twelve
Symphonie fantastique, Op. 14,
2nd movement, 'Un bal'
Orchestre National de France
Conducted by James Conlon
℗ Erato Classics SNC, Paris,
France 1984

5. Setting off on his travels
Harold en Italie, Op. 16,
3rd movement, 'Sérénade
d'un montagnard des Abruzzes
à sa maîtresse'
Claude Ducrocq, viola
Orchestre Philharmonique
de Strasbourg
Conducted by Alain Lombard
℗ Erato Classics SNC, Paris,
France 1973

6. The love of singing
La Captive, Op. 12
Catherine Robbin, mezzo-soprano
Orchestre de l'Opéra de Lyon
Conducted by John Eliot Gardiner
2292 45517 2
℗ Erato Classics SNC, Paris,
France 1990
Co-production Erato/Radio France/
Opéra de Lyon/Rhône Poulenc

7. Night and nightmares
Symphonie fantastique, Op. 14,
5th movement, 'Songe d'une nuit
de sabbat'
Orchestre National de France
Conducted by James Conlon
℗ Erato Classics SNC, Paris,
France 1984

8. Opera
Les Troyens, Act 5,
Dido: 'Je vais mourir'
Françoise Pollet, soprano
Orchestre Philharmonique
de Montpellier
Conducted by Cyril Diederich
2292 45025 2
℗ Erato Classics SNC, Paris,
France 1990
Co-production Erato/Radio France

9. Symphonic music
Symphonie fantastique, Op. 14,
4th movement, 'Marche au supplice'
Orchestre National de France

Conducted by James Conlon
℗ Erato Classics SNC, Paris,
France 1984

Harold en Italie, Op. 16,
2nd movement, 'Marche des pèlerins
chantant la prière du soir'
Claude Ducrocq, viola
Orchestre Philharmonique
de Strasbourg
Conducted by Alain Lombard
℗ Erato Classics SNC, Paris,
France 1973

IO. Sacred music
L'Enfance du Christ, Op. 25,
'La Fuite en Égypte', Overture
Orchestre de l'Opéra de Lyon
Conducted by John Eliot Gardiner
2292 45275 2
℗ Erato Classics SNC, Paris,
France 1988
Co-production Erato/Cascavelle/
France Musique/Opéra de Lyon

II. Strange works
La Damnation de Faust, Op. 24,
'La Course à l'abîme': 'Dans mon
coeur retentit sa voix désespérée'
Thomas Moser, tenor
José Van Dam, baritone
Choeur et Orchestre de l'Opéra de Lyon
Conducted by Kent Nagano
0630 10692 2
℗ Erato Disques S.A., Paris, France
1995
Co-production Erato/Opéra de Lyon

Les Nuits d'été, Op. 7,
'L'Île inconnue'
Diane Montague, mezzo-soprano
Orchestre de l'Opéra de Lyon
Conducted by John Eliot Gardiner§
2292 45517 2
℗ Erato Classics SNC, Paris,
France 1990
Co-production Erato/Radio France/
Opéra de Lyon/Rhône Poulenc

JOHANN SEBASTIAN BACH
LUDWIG VAN BEETHOVEN
HECTOR BERLIOZ
FRYDERYK CHOPIN
CLAUDE DEBUSSY
GEORGE FRIDERIC HANDEL
WOLFGANG AMADEUS MOZART
HENRY PURCELL
FRANZ SCHUBERT
ANTONIO VIVALDI